Spilling the Beans on...

Julius Caesar

and his friends, Romans and countrymen

First published in 2000 by Miles Kelly Publishing,
Bardfield Centre, Great Bardfield, Essex CM7 4SL

Printed in China

This edition printed in 2008

ISBN 978-1-902947-19-8

4 6 8 10 9 7 5

Cover design and illustration: Inc
Layout design: GQ
Art Direction: Clare Sleven

Spilling the Beans on...

Julius Caesar

and his friends, Romans and countrymen

by Mick Gowar

Illustrations Mike Mosedale

ABOUT THE AUTHOR

Mick Gowar has written or edited over 40 books for children, including collections of poetry, novels, graphic novels, picture books, short stories, and four books about life in Roman times. He has visited over 600 schools, libraries, colleges and other venues to give talks and performances of his work, or to lead workshops. As well as writing and performing, he is at present a part-time lecture in the Department of Illustration and Graphic Arts at Anglia University, Cambridge.

CONTENTS

FAMILY ALBUM

Julius Caesar was born in Rome in 100BC. His father was a not very successful politician, but Caesar came from a very grand family. Caesar's family tree includes:

- at least two murderers
- two murder victims
- six soldiers
- two major gods.

Caesar followed in the family footsteps – he became all four.

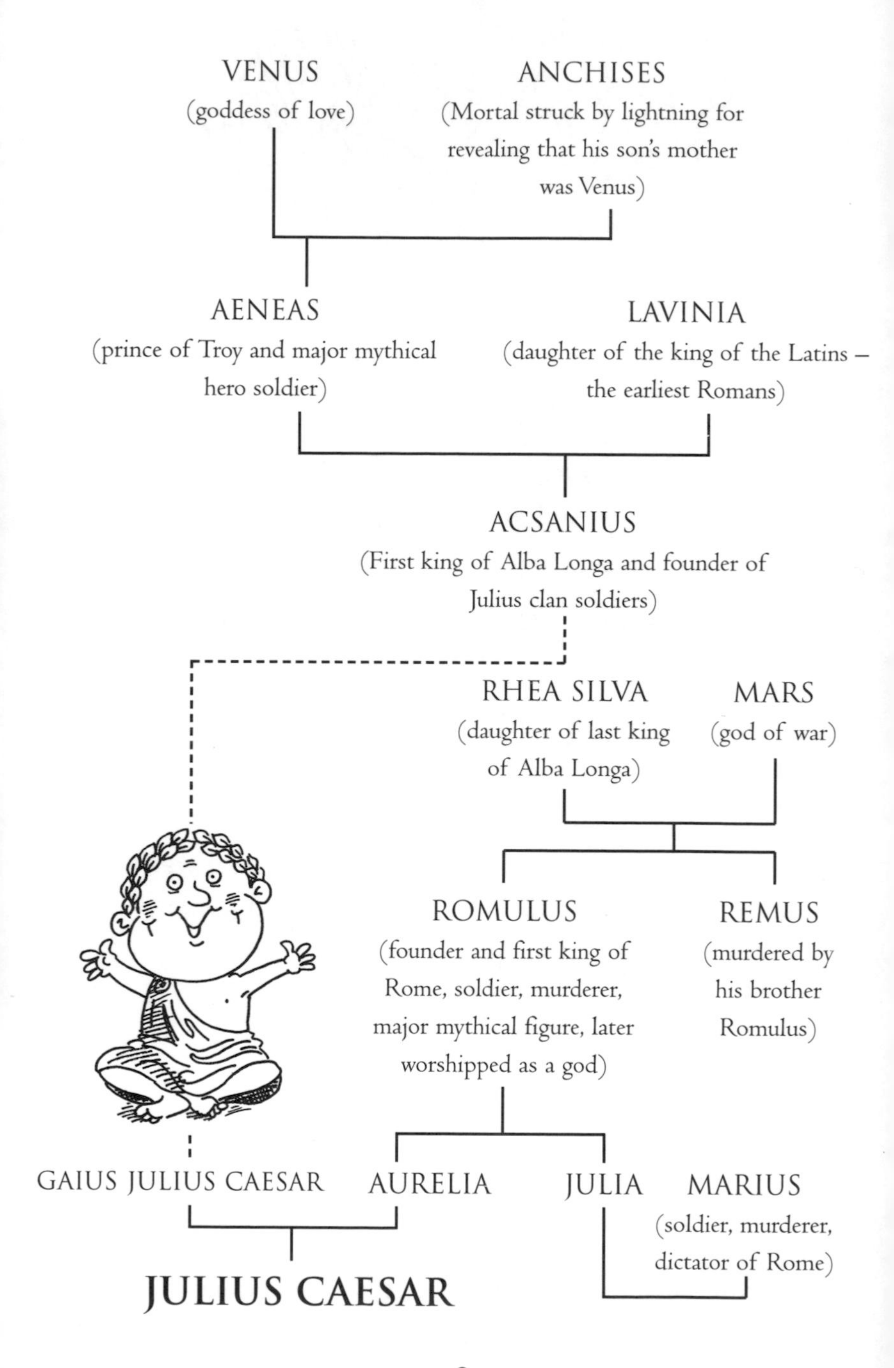
VENUS
(goddess of love)
ANCHISES
(Mortal struck by lightning for revealing that his son's mother was Venus)
AENEAS
(prince of Troy and major mythical hero soldier)
LAVINIA
(daughter of the king of the Latins – the earliest Romans)
ACSANIUS
(First king of Alba Longa and founder of Julius clan soldiers)
RHEA SILVA
(daughter of last king of Alba Longa)
MARS
(god of war)
ROMULUS
(founder and first king of Rome, soldier, murderer, major mythical figure, later worshipped as a god)
REMUS
(murdered by his brother Romulus)
GAIUS JULIUS CAESAR
AURELIA
JULIA
MARIUS
(soldier, murderer, dictator of Rome)
JULIUS CAESAR

HOME TOWN

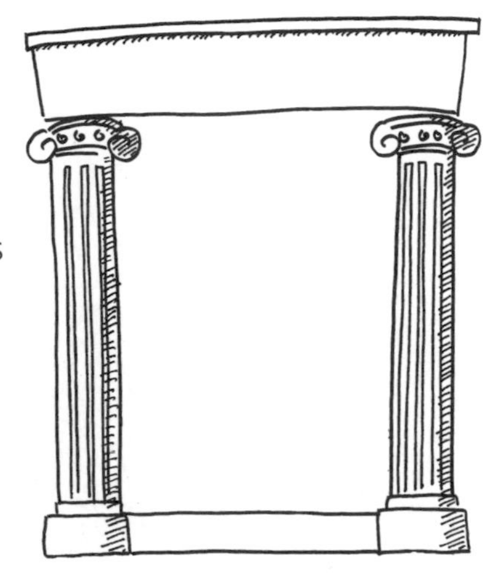

Rome in 100BC was the biggest and most important city in the world, and Caesar's family was one of the oldest and most respected families in Rome. Caesar's father was a senator, a member of the council or parliament of wealthy Romans who ran the Roman empire.

Rome at this time did not have an emperor or a king. The Roman empire was a republic – that means it was a nation without a monarch. Every year the Senate elected two consuls whose jobs were to be something like joint prime ministers for a year. The other ministers were elected, too.

All male citizens present in Rome at the time of an election could vote. In cases of emergency – like war or revolution – the Senate could appoint a dictator (a supreme commander) to take charge, but only for six months.

The baby Caesar would one day change all that. Although he would never have the title, he would grow up to be, in all but name, the first Roman emperor.

FAMILY STORIES

No-one knew exactly when the city of Rome was founded, but there were a number of stories which children like the young Caesar were told. One of these stories told how twins Romulus and Remus were left to die when they were babies by their wicked uncle. A wild wolf found them and brought them up. When they were adults, and Romulus started to build a city, Remus made fun of him by jumping over the city walls. Romulus got so cross that he lost his temper and killed his brother. Romulus carried on building his city which he named after himself – Rome. This was an important story for Caesar's family because Caesar's mother claimed to be directly descended from Romulus.

But an even more important story to the Caesar family was the story of Aeneas. Caesar's father claimed descent back to Aeneas himself, the great hero and a son of a goddess. Aeneas, a prince from the city of Troy, had sailed to Italy and founded a kingdom which was the beginning of the Roman empire.

Here's the story that Caesar would have been told when he was a child, about Aeneas and the Trojan War. It's one of the oldest and strangest stories in the world.

THE TROJAN WAR AND PRINCE AENEAS

Over a thousand years before you (Caesar) were born, a great war was fought at a city called Troy (it's on the coast of what is now Turkey).

The war started when Paris, one of the sons of the King of Troy, kidnapped Helen, the wife of Menelaus who was the King of a town called Sparta in Greece. Paris took Helen back to Troy to be his wife.

Menelaus was very annoyed because:

(a) Helen was young.
(b) Helen was very beautiful.
(c) Menelaus was old, ugly and bad-tempered and was very unlikely to find a wife as good-looking as Helen again.
(d) Menelaus was very proud, and knew he'd been made to look a fool.

Helen didn't mind being kidnapped. Helen was in love with Paris because:

(a) Paris was young.
(b) Paris was handsome.
(c) Paris was being helped by Venus, the goddess of love – sneaky Paris!

Menelaus persuaded the other Greek kings like

Agamemnon, King of Athens – the most powerful man in the world; Odysseus, King of Ithaca – the cleverest man in the world; and Achilles, King of the Myrmidons – the best fighter in the world; to help him start a war to get Helen back. (The Spartans were famous for wanting to solve every problem by fighting).

You would have thought with a team like that, it wouldn't have taken long to get Helen back. So did the Greeks. They were wrong.

The Greek army sailed to Troy, then they camped outside the city walls and waited for the Trojans to get:

(a) scared
(b) hungry
(c) bored

and give Helen back.

They waited... and they waited... and they waited. Every few days, some Trojan soldiers would leave the city and fight some of the Greek soldiers.

But when it got dark, the Trojans went home to their city and the Greeks went back to their camp.

This went on for ten years, until Odysseus had a brilliant idea.

One morning the Trojans woke up to find that the Greeks had sailed away. All that was left, where the Greek camp had been, was an enormous wooden horse.

What a trophy! The biggest toy horse in the world! The triumphant Trojans dragged the horse into the city, and began the celebrations.

That night, when all the Trojans were either asleep or drunk, a trapdoor opened in the horse and out climbed a troop of Greek soldiers. They crept to the gates of the city and opened them.

The Greek army was outside waiting for the gates to open. They hadn't sailed away, but just sailed out of sight.

They burnt Troy to the ground, killing the men and boys, and carrying off the women as slaves.

Well... they didn't kill all the men. Aeneas, Paris's cousin and the son of the goddess Venus, escaped on a boat with a handful of followers. They sailed to Italy, where Aeneas married Lavinia, the daughter of the king of the Latins.

Aeneas and Lavinia had a son, Ascanius, who founded the city of Alba Longa, from which grew the whole Roman empire. Ascanius also took the family name of 'Julius'.

So that was the story. You probably noticed that Aeneas was supposed to have been the son of the goddess Venus. That was why Caesar's family not only claimed they were the descendants of Aeneas, but also claimed to be related to the goddess Venus, too.

BABY IN DANGER

The Romans had many customs which we would say were cruel, and because of one of these customs, Caesar's life was in great danger as soon as he was born.

According to an ancient tradition, Caesar's mother, Aurelia, had to lay her new-born baby at his father's feet. If Caesar's father picked him up, everything was fine; if he refused, the baby would be taken to a public place like the side of a road – and left. If a kind-hearted passer-by didn't pick up the baby it would die within hours.

For a moment or two there must have been an anxious silence in the room, until... Gaius picked up his son!

Nine days later, Caesar's parents held a naming ceremony, which is similar to a christening. Friends and relatives of Gaius and Aurelia came to the house with gifts, incense was burnt, the baby was bathed and then given his name: Gaius Julius Caesar, just like his father. *Gaius* was his personal name like Gary, or Michael or Peter. *Julius* was the old family name, the clan name for everyone – cousins, second cousins, third and fourth cousins and so on – who claimed to be related to Aeneas and his son.

Caesar was the surname of their particular family, and it comes from an ancient word for *elephant*. There was a story behind that too.

A hundred years before Caesar was born, a general called Hannibal invaded Italy. Hannibal came from a place called Carthage, in North Africa, and as well as bringing lots of soldiers with him – a good idea if you're fighting a war – he brought with him a secret weapon which he hoped would absolutely *terrify* the Romans – battle elephants!

One of Caesar's ancestors had single-handedly killed one of Hannibal's elephants in a battle and had either taken or been given the name *Caesar* – the elephant killer. The name stuck, as nicknames often do, and became his family name.

GROWING UP ROMAN

When he was a baby and a toddler Caesar was looked after by a nurse, just as rich children today may be looked after by a nanny or nursery maid.

Then, when he was seven, Caesar started his schooling. But Caesar never went to school. He took all his lessons at home.

Caesar's first teachers were his parents. His mother taught him to read and write both Latin and Greek. Latin was the language of the Romans, but Greek was very important too, because a lot of Roman culture – art, history, philosophy and religion – had been taken from the Greeks. She also taught him his first lessons in public speaking.

Public speaking, or to give it its Greek name, *rhetoric,* was a very important part of any aristocratic Roman's education. All the best jobs in Rome – like being Consul – were elected. To get a good job, you had to be able to persuade people to vote for you. Rhetoric was the art of persuasion.

Caesar's father taught him physical skills like wrestling, throwing the javelin and discus, and swimming. But these weren't simply sports; this was training for the army. Caesar's father knew that, like all high-born Romans, someday young Caesar would join the army. The skills he learnt as a boy might someday be the difference between life and death.

Young Caesar was a natural athlete, and he especially enjoyed riding. When he was in his early teens he often spent his afternoons, after his lessons had finished, at a huge sports ground called the *Campus Martius.* Caesar was a bit of a show-off and used to ride across the sports ground as fast as he could with no hands.

After a few years of lessons from his parents, young Caesar started lessons with a tutor, a Greek slave who taught him grammar, literature, and more classes on how to win friends and influence people through making speeches.

This seems a good place to tell you about...

SLAVES, PLEBS, KNIGHTS AND PATRICIANS

In ancient Rome there were rules and customs for everything, and everyone belonged to one of four classes.

Patricians – top dogs

At the top were the families like Caesar's who were known as *patricians*. They were similar to the old 'noble' families of Britain – the dukes, earls and lords. They had land and money, and some had the right by birth to a place in the Senate (like British aristocrats used to have a seat in Parliament in the House of Lords). The patricians believed they had a right to run the country. They also thought that doing ordinary jobs was for the lower orders. Like the Caesar family, the other patrician families claimed they were descended from the original founders of Rome.

Equites (knights) – almost pedigree dogs

The *equites* were the descendants of the first Roman cavalry officers, but by Caesar's time they had nothing to do with horses. Equite was just a title, like a modern British knighthood (no-one expects Sir Elton John or Sir Paul McCartney to ride around on horseback wearing armour, although the title comes from a time when that's what knights did).

Like many British knights today, Roman equites in Caesar's time were businessmen – rich merchants, bankers and money-lenders. Patricians thought it was beneath them to lend money, but they were only too happy to borrow it – often vast sums. During Caesar's lifetime, the equites were becoming more and more powerful. Equites could be elected to the Senate.

Plebeians – working dogs

These were the ordinary working people, craftsmen and shop keepers. They were full citizens and could vote in elections. They also elected two special representatives called *tribunes* who could veto any law passed by the Senate. That meant that if a tribune didn't like a law it would be thrown out. No-one else in Rome had the power to overrule the Senate.

Slaves – mutts and curs

It may seem strange that an important family like Caesar's would have had their son educated by a slave, but that's how things were done in Rome. Slaves did an awful lot of the work.

As you might expect, slaves did all the hard, horrible jobs that no-one else wanted to do, like mining or breaking rocks in quarries. There were household slaves to do all the housework like cooking and cleaning. By the time Caesar was a boy, more and more jobs in Rome were done by slaves. A lot of what we would call 'office workers' – secretaries, clerks and accountants – were slaves. Slaves also did jobs which we would call 'professional' – most librarians, teachers and doctors were also slaves. And entertainers, like dancers and singers, were slaves too. Slaves earned money, and if they saved enough they could buy their freedom.

But however trusted and even well-paid a slave was, he or she was not regarded as a person, but as the property of their master. And that master could, in theory, do what he liked with them. Sometimes they did. Pliny, a Roman writer recorded:

> **Vedius Pollio [a friend of Caesar's nephew] practised his barbarity with the assistance of moray eels, into whose tank he threw condemned slaves... because with no other living creature could he watch a man being torn to pieces utterly and instantaneously.**

Slave marriages were not recognised, and any children born to slaves automatically became slaves themselves. Although masters as cruel as Vedius Pollio were rare, Roman law laid down brutal punishments for slaves who committed crimes. If, for example, a slave killed his master, even someone as cruel as Vedius Pollio, *all* the slaves in the house would be executed.

UNEMPLOYED – DOGS FOR SALE

Because so many jobs were done by slaves, lots of plebeians, equites and even patricians had no work and no money. During Caesar's lifetime there were about 500,000 people living in Rome. Around 130,000 people received free food – what the Romans called the *corn dole.* These would have been plebeians. The higher class unemployed would have taken up being 'clients'. Clients were what might be called high class scroungers, living on what they could get as handouts from rich senators. Every rich man had a group of clients, and every client had a 'patron', a particular rich man who looked after him.

Everyday at dawn, a huge army of clients would put on their togas and start queuing outside the houses of their patrons. The queue would be in strict order of class: patrician relatives of the rich man first, followed by non-related patricians, then equites and so on. When the rich man came out – to go to the Senate, for example – he would give out gifts of money or even food, to his clients.

Why did the rich man do this? Out of kindness? No. The clients, and the unemployed plebeians on the corn dole, had something a rich and powerful man needed in order to stay rich: **VOTES.**

The unemployed plebeians and the higher-class clients were all citizens and therefore had the right to vote in the elections for all the top jobs. In return for being a patron, the rich man got the votes of his clients. It was as simple as that.

A rich man could also try to buy the votes of the plebeians, by voting for increases in the corn dole, and paying for the entertainments – like gladiator fights, or fights between men and exotic wild animals – that filled the days of the un- and underemployed. The Romans used to call this giving the people "bread and circuses". Any patrician who seemed to stand up for the common man, especially of the idle sort, could have a huge number of votes in his pocket. The only trouble was, it all cost a *fortune!*

ADULT LIFE STARTS WITH A TOGA

When he was fifteen, Caesar's father gave him his *toga virilis* – his adult toga. This was a big day in a boy's life. Like an 18th birthday nowadays, or graduation from school or college, it was the start of adult life.

The toga was a huge piece of circular woollen cloth, like an enormous curved blanket. It was five-and-a-half metres wide, and was worn draped and folded over a tunic. The toga was so big that it was virtually impossible to put on without the help of at least one slave, and it was usually worn with only a belt to hold it together. It was a major problem to walk, or move in any way, without the whole thing coming unwrapped.

bad Toga day!

It was the official dress – the business suit or uniform – of the adult male Roman citizen, and only *full* citizens of the Roman empire were allowed to wear it.

Senators were allowed to wear a toga with a purple stripe along the edge to show their rank, rather like a corporal or sergeant in the army now wears stripes to show they're above the ordinary soldier.

When a boy got his toga it showed that he'd become a man, and the day he received it there would be a mixture of a party and a religious celebration.

Caesar's special day started with friends and relations coming to the house to congratulate him and give him presents. Then Caesar walked with his father to the temple of Jupiter, made a sacrifice and was officially proclaimed a full citizen of the Roman Empire.

Caesar was very keen on fashion, and soon developed his own form of the toga. He added wrist-length fringed sleeves and always wore his belt very slack. One of his family's greatest political enemies, Sulla, when seeing Caesar wearing his fancy toga, was heard to mutter: 'Beware of that boy with his loose clothes.'

MORE TO BEING A GROWN-UP THAN JUST A BLANKET

There was only one way for a boy of Caesar's class to get on in Rome, and that was to go into politics.

None of the best jobs in the Roman Empire – as a lawyer or judge, top civil servant, religious leader or senior officer in the army – were permanent jobs. They were all elected for short terms. (In the same way that today, in the United States, jobs like district attorney, chief-of-police, sheriff or fire-chief in towns and cities are also elected. The commander-in-chief of the US army is also elected – that's the president.) Nowadays we think of these as separate careers, needing particular skills and training. But in Caesar's day, an aristocratic Roman would move from one job to another without thinking too much about it.

He might start out as a junior lawyer, then go into the army – as an officer, of course. After a year or two in the army, he might try a year as a judge or a junior minister.

Then, if he bribed enough people, he could get elected as a religious leader, even a chief priest, or he could then go back into the army, this time as a general. If he fought a successful war, and if he was really lucky, he might come back to Rome and be elected as one of the two consuls who were chosen every year to rule the empire.

Does that sound strange? Well, that was the sort of career that ambitious young Romans like Caesar hoped for.

So in order to get one of these jobs, Caesar had to become a politician. And at the age of 15, with a family like his, Caesar might have assumed success was guaranteed. But it wasn't.

A BRIGHT START

Success for a patrician didn't depend on how clever you were, but on who your family and friends were. Did you have a rich father, or uncle who could help you buy the votes you needed? Did you have a father-in-law or older brother who could call in favours in order to get you the job you wanted?

We would say today, and quite rightly, that the whole system was completely rotten and corrupt. But for the Romans this was how things had always been, and as far as they were concerned this was how things always would be.

Caesar's father wasn't rich or powerful, but his Uncle Marius, who was married to Caesar's Aunt Julia, was the most powerful man in the whole Roman empire.

MARIUS

Uncle Marius was a very unusual man. He wasn't born a patrician, but had worked his way up through the army through sheer ability and ruthlessness. Uncle Marius was brilliant, Uncle Marius was charming, and Uncle Marius was quite prepared to use murder to get his way if his brilliance and his charm didn't get him what he wanted.

Marius had utterly transformed the Roman army. Until Marius became a general, only people who owned land and had enough money to provide all their own equipment were allowed to join the army. Marius changed the rules so that any citizen could join. Soldiers now had their equipment provided for them, had reasonable pay, and the promise of a pension – either money or a small plot of land – when they finished their twenty years service.

Suddenly, thousands of unemployed men could have a job, a wage, and the hope of a secure future for themselves and their families by joining the army. The ordinary people thought Marius was great, especially as he claimed to be one of them. And the soldiers in his army were so grateful, they would follow him to hell and back.

Marius became not just a soldier, but one of the most powerful politicians in the empire. He was the leader of a group of senators called the *populares* who claimed to be the champions of the ordinary people. Caesar's father was a *popularis*, too.

But powerful men make powerful enemies, and Marius had made a very powerful enemy, a man named Sulla. Sulla had once been Marius's lieutenant, but had later become one of the leaders of the other main group in the Senate, the *optimates.* The optimates supported the aristocrats, not the ordinary people. They tried to pass laws to give more power to the patricians – the land-owners and the rich.

Then in 87BC, when Caesar was 13, Marius and his ally Cinna seized power in Rome while Sulla was away fighting in Greece. Marius was appointed dictator and at once ordered the execution of Sulla's main supporters.

Sulla was a powerful man, with a long memory. But Sulla was in exile a long way away. For Marius's family and friends – including Caesar and his family – the future looked bright.

DISASTERS FOR CAESAR

Caesar's father should have helped him on his way to the start of his career, but just before Caesar was 16 his father died. Caesar was now the head of his family. Soon after, there was another loss for the family, when Marius died too.

Caesar wasn't sure what to do, or where to turn for the help his father and his uncle would have given him. Then Aunt Julia stepped in.

Marius's widow was a very strong woman; no-one argued with Aunt Julia. Young Caesar was already engaged to be married to Cossetta, the daughter of a wealthy equite who could lend Caesar the money he needed to get a start in politics. But that was nothing compared to what Aunt Julia had in mind.

Caesar didn't marry Cossetta. Cossetta got dumped. Instead Caesar married Cornelia, the daughter of Cinna, Uncle Marius's old ally and now the most powerful man in Rome.

A brilliant future now seemed certain for young Caesar. Then, another disaster – his father-in-law Cinna was killed in Spain during a mutiny of his troops.

During the time that Marius and Cinna were in power, Sulla had been in exile, waiting for his chance. This was it. Sulla didn't hesitate. Within days he'd marched back to Rome and seized power. Caesar was in deep trouble.

If success depended on family connections rather than anything you did, so could your life. Sulla was back, and he had a list of everyone he considered an enemy: anyone who had opposed him, or anyone who was related to them. Caesar was Marius's nephew and Cinna's son-in-law. To Sulla, even though Caesar was hardly more than a boy, he was one of the most dangerous men in Rome. Caesar was arrested immediately and taken to Sulla.

Sulla had set up his headquarters in the temple of the war goddess Bellona. Not far away, on the Campus Martius, supporters of Marius were being put to death. Their screams could clearly be heard from the room in which

Caesar was questioned. Imagine how frightening this must have been for Caesar. Would he be the next to be marched out to the Campus Martius?

But instead of condemning him immediately, Sulla offered Caesar a deal. "Join me," he said, "and, to show you're on my side, divorce your wife and I'll pick you a new one."

Ninety-nine out of a hundred Romans, with their life in such danger, would have taken Sulla's offer. Not Caesar. He refused.

Sulla must have been astonished at the teenager's refusal, because he didn't have him killed at once. Instead, he confiscated everything that Caesar and his wife owned and let Caesar go.

It didn't take Sulla long to have second thoughts. He declared Caesar an outlaw, with a price on his head. But when the first bounty hunters arrived at his house to kill him, Caesar was gone.

ON THE RUN

This is what the Roman writer Appian said in his book on the civil wars:

> Sulla... pronounced a sentence of death on forty senators and about 1,600 knights... Very soon he added other senators to the list. Some of them, caught unawares, were killed where they were found; at home, in the street, or in the temple... Others were dragged through the streets and kicked to death,

the spectators being too frightened to utter a word of protest at the horrors they witnessed. Others were expelled from Rome or had their property and belongings confiscated. Spies were looking everywhere for those who had fled the city, and killing any they caught leaving.

For a whole year Caesar was in hiding in the countryside outside Rome. He often had to go from one hiding place to another at night to avoid Sulla's spies who were looking for him. During this time Caesar became so ill with malaria that he sometimes had to be carried from one hiding place to another by friends.

Once, he was actually caught by a group of Sulla's men, but managed to borrow enough money to bribe them to go away.

Meanwhile in Rome, his mother, his wife and the rest of his family were begging Sulla to let him come back. Eventually, Sulla gave in. But Caesar didn't trust Sulla. Instead of coming home to Rome, Caesar joined the army and didn't return to Rome until 78BC when he got news that Sulla was dead.

ARMY LIFE

The Roman army was divided into legions, roughly equivalent to the regiments of the modern British army. Each legion had a number and title – for example *The Ninth Hispania* – and each legion had a standard, a silver eagle which was carried into battle with them. If the enemy captured the eagle it was a great disgrace, and the legion would be disbanded if they couldn't win it back.

Each legion was made up of nine cohorts of 480 men each. Caesar's first job would have been as the officer in charge of a cohort.

Even in peacetime, army life was tough. Every day the troops had to practice swimming, running and javelin throwing, and every couple of weeks they would have to march at least thirty kilometres in a day at speeds of up to eight kilometres per hour.

SPQR

Fighting wasn't the only job of the legions. They were also responsible for building roads and bridges. So as well as all their weapons, food and cooking pots, each soldier had to carry digging tools with him.

Caesar's Uncle Marius invented a forked pole to help the legionnaires carry all their equipment. It may have helped the soldiers, but it got them the nickname "Marius's mules".

Many people hated life in the army, but Caesar loved it. He was strong and fit, and discovered that not only was he a good fighter, but he was a natural leader – other soldiers respected him and would willingly follow him.

HARD LESSONS

The Caesar who came home to Rome in 78BC wasn't a boy any more. He was only in his early twenties, but he was a tough survivor. He'd survived a civil war, he'd survived being an outlaw on the run, and he'd not just survived but *enjoyed* the tough life of the army. He'd seen the violence and killing of Sulla's dictatorship, and could probably remember the killings which his Uncle Marius had ordered when he'd seized control of Rome. If what he'd learned had to be summed up in one phrase it was: *trust no-one, especially not the Senate.*

Caesar knew that the only safe place to be was at the very top. And that's where he decided he was going.

To get to the top in Roman politics took money, *lots* of money. Caesar needed money to bribe senators, money to bribe equites, and money to bribe the ordinary people of

Rome. But that wasn't all. Caesar knew that to get to the top he needed soldiers who would do *anything* he asked them to do – that was another lesson he'd learnt from his Uncle Marius. That took money too. But Caesar didn't have money. What could he do?

Easy: he borrowed. He borrowed a fortune, from anyone who would lend it to him. He even borrowed money to make himself look rich, so that he could borrow *even more* money.

"Lend me money now, and when I'm the most powerful man in Rome you'll get back hundreds of times the value of what you lend me today!" – that was the deal that Caesar offered. The tough young man must have been convincing, because there were plenty of Romans willing to lend money to young Caesar.

The first thing Caesar did was to try and make his name as a lawyer and a public speaker. He lost both his first cases, but made such an impression that the accused men hired the best lawyers in Rome to defend themselves against him.

Caesar was now famous. Among lawyers and politicians, he was famous as a brilliant lawyer and speaker. Among ordinary people he was famous for his generosity to his clients and the lavish parties he threw (with borrowed money, of course). If there had been gossip columns in Rome, Caesar would have been in them every day:

Another wild night at the home of free-spending young swinger, Gaius Julius Caesar.

Having made a name for himself as a lawyer with a big future, Caesar was throwing another of his extravagant parties – this time to say farewell to a few close friends before setting sail for Greece.

Caesar hasn't gotta lotta loot, but he still manages to push the boat out – using other people's cash!

But one thing's for sure, Caesar's got his eye on the top job. So, it'll be spend, spend, spend – and lend, lend, lend – for this partying patrician!

But Caesar's creditors, the people who had lent him money, were getting impatient; so impatient that some of them were asking for their money back *or else.*

Caesar gave the moneylenders the slip, and sailed for Greece. Greece was a good choice. He'd become famous by standing up for Greeks against corrupt Roman officials, and certain Greeks had hinted that they might reward Caesar with what Caesar needed most – money. Greece also had the best teachers of rhetoric. While in Greece, Caesar hoped to study with one of them. The next time he went to court, he *wasn't* going to lose again.

Everything was looking good; everything was going to plan. The boat was making good progress, only a couple more days and... Caesar looked out to sea. Other ships were approaching fast. Pirate ships.

CAPTURED BY PIRATES

The Mediterranean Sea at this time was being terrorised by pirates. They would stop ships and steal their cargoes, and any wealthy passengers would be held to ransom. That's what happened to Caesar.

Most people would have been terrified at being captured

by pirates, but Caesar seemed to treat the whole experience as a huge joke. Plutarch, the Greek historian, wrote:

When the pirates demanded a ransom of twenty talents Caesar burst out laughing. They did not know, he said, who it was they had captured – and he volunteered to pay them fifty.

The pirates let some of Caesar's companions go ashore to start collecting the ransom money. Caesar, of course, stayed behind as a hostage.

Even then, with his friends gone, Caesar didn't seem in the least bit nervous. He treated the pirates like servants. Once, when his afternoon nap was disturbed, he yelled at the pirates to be quiet.

> For 38 days... he joined in all their games and exercises, just as if he were their leader instead of their prisoner. He also wrote poems and speeches which he read aloud to them, and if they failed to admire his work, he would call them illiterate savages to their faces, and would often laughingly threaten to have them all hanged.

Caesar may have been laughing, but he wasn't joking. Caesar was a proud man, and he was planning to be a successful soldier and politician. He couldn't be seen to come off second best to a group of pirates.

When the ransom was paid and Caesar was freed, he immediately borrowed even more money, chartered a small fleet of ships, found the pirates and captured them.

He took them ashore and demanded justice from the local Greek magistrates. When the magistrates dithered – maybe because they were afraid of the pirates – Caesar marched the prisoners out and crucified them all. (But because he'd enjoyed their company, he had them strangled first rather than leave them to a slow, agonising death. That was Caesar's idea of mercy.)

Maybe this adventure shows another of the lessons Caesar may have learned from Marius and Sulla: *Never let anyone get the better of you, and treat any enemy without mercy.*

Caesar returned to Rome. The story of his adventures with the pirates added to his growing reputation. Here was a young man, people said, who was not only a good lawyer, but was brave, strong and ruthless. The sort of person, they whispered, that Rome needed to bring order to the chaos caused by the bickering, back-stabbing, indecisive senators.

ROME IN TURMOIL

The Senate had never been designed to run an empire. It was a town council which, by accident, found itself trying to run half the world. Rome was in a dreadful mess.

More and more people came to Rome looking for work and finding none. The most important jobs in government were bought and sold, while the generals who commanded the armies overseas became more and more powerful, and more and more ambitious.

The Senate desperately need to reorganise itself, but the two groups or parties – the *optimates* and the *populares* – had utterly opposite views of what needed to be done. "More power to the rich and powerful!" yelled the optimates.

Keep the Optimates and Populares supporters separate - we don't want crowd trouble.
SENATE

"More power to the people!" bellowed the populares. There was no agreement, so nothing changed.

Elections had become street battles between the supporters of rival candidates. Plutarch, a Greek writer, wrote:

> **Candidates for office quite shamelessly bribed the electorate... people who received bribes went down to the Forum [the main square in Rome where elections were held] not so much to vote for their benefactors as to fight for them with bows and arrows and swords and slings. Often, before an election was over, the place where it had been held was stained with blood and defiled with dead bodies.**

Caesar borrowed more and more money and bribed more and more important people to try and get a really important job. And when money wasn't enough to win over an important backer, Caesar was quite prepared to crawl and fawn. According to Cassius Dio, a Roman historian:

"Caesar showed himself perfectly ready to serve and flatter everybody, even ordinary persons... he did not mind temporarily grovelling."

But all the bribery and flattery worked: Caesar got the job he wanted, as a *quaestor,* one of twenty magistrates and administrators who helped to run the empire. Caesar was sent to Spain to help the Roman governor.

But not everything was going well. Cornelia died before he was due to go to Spain. Caesar was without a wife, and his young daughter Julia had lost her mother.

ONWARDS AND UPWARDS

The job of Quaestor didn't just give Caesar experience of helping to run an important part of the empire. With the job, came a seat in the Senate – for life. When Caesar came back to Rome after his year abroad, he was at last one of the most important men in the empire.

He married again. His new wife was Pompeia, the wealthy granddaughter of his former arch-enemy, Sulla. He now had contacts and friends on both sides of the Senate, although he remained a populare all his life. He also had a new source of money – his new wife's fortune.

Pompeia may have brought Caesar an enormous dowry (the money a bride gave to her husband on marriage) but the way Caesar spent it, no amount of money seemed to last long. Especially with the new job Caesar now got, the post of *aedile.*

BREAD AND CIRCUSES

One of the main jobs of an aedile was to organise the games and entertainments which filled the time of the vast mob of unemployed and underemployed people who filled the streets of Rome. It would be like being in charge of all television, radio and film-making today. For any rising Roman politician, but especially a popularis like Caesar, getting the job of one of the four aediles was crucial for building a reputation as a friend of the people and buying their votes.

Many entertainments which were very popular in ancient Rome we would think of as horrible today. Slaves and criminals were specially trained to fight each other to the death; these were the famous *gladiators.* The best gladiators became superstars and made fortunes – enough to buy their freedom and set up their own gladiator schools. Wild animals would be made to fight and kill each other, or be 'hunted' around the arena by teams of slaves.

Caesar spent vast amounts of borrowed money on the most amazing circuses and games that anyone had ever seen. He paid to have gladiators dressed in solid silver armour. And instead of the usual gladiator fights, he had one arena filled with water and staged a 'sea-battle' with the gladiators fighting each other from ships.

To impress his fellow senators, Caesar decorated his house with the most expensive works of art. He even built a huge country house, then as soon as it was finished he had it pulled down because he didn't like it after all.

Caesar was living the life of a multi-millionaire, but it was all a sham. Caesar was in more debt than he'd ever been in his life before. He owed so much money to so many people, that even he didn't know if he'd ever be able to pay it back again. Unless he got a really important a job – a job where he could start taking bribes instead of paying them out – Caesar was going to be in big trouble.

DON'T CALL HIM BALDY

According to his biographers, Caesar at this time was tall, slim and broad-faced. He had a high-pitched voice and was *very* proud of his appearance.

Unfortunately, he'd started going bald when he was only in his twenties and, being vain, tried to hide it by growing his hair long at the back and combing it forward to try and hide his bald patch. As Caesar got older, and even the hair at the back started to get thinner and thinner, this must have looked more and more silly. By the end of his life, he employed four personal barbers who would all work at the same time to arrange his hair to try and hide his baldness.

His political opponents used to make jokes about it, which Caesar hated... Suetonius, who wrote a book about Caesar, claimed: "Of all the honours voted him by the Senate and people, none pleased him so much as the privilege of wearing a laurel wreath on all occasions." I expect you can guess why.

But his vanity could make opponents underestimate Caesar. Cicero, one of his political enemies, admitted:

"When I notice how carefully arranged his hair is and when I watch him adjusting the parting with one finger, I cannot imagine that this man could conceive of such a wicked crime as to destroy the Roman Republic."

SMOOTH OPERATOR?

Strangely, for someone so obsessed with hair loss, Caesar used to have all his body hair plucked out with tweezers. *Ouch!* This would have been done while he bathed. Caesar, like many Romans, was very keen on taking baths.

Roman baths were not just a quick wash down in hot water. Romans took *hours* to bathe.

Roman baths were much more like what we would call saunas or Turkish baths, followed by a work-out in a gym or fitness centre.

Caesar's body hair.
retain for possible re-use on head.

The idea wasn't to wash yourself clean, but to sweat yourself clean, starting in a hot steam room called a *calderium* and then going on to a *really* hot room called a *sudatoria.* While you were sweating, a slave would scrape all the gunk and muck off your body with a special long-bladed knife called a *strigel.*

After the steaming and strigelling, you would plunge into a freezing cold pool called a *frigiderium.* And then, if you were still feeling grimy, you could do it all over again.

As well as cleaning yourself, there were masseurs to give you a massage if you felt a bit stiff and achey, and gym equipment like weights and heavy lead-filled balls to lift to give yourself a work-out.

One of the things which made Caesar popular with ordinary Romans, were the baths he paid for. Not only did he pay for them to be built, but he also made sure that the price of admission was incredibly low. Thanks to Caesar, even the poorest Roman could afford to go to the baths and be boiled, frozen and have all his or her body hairs plucked out – just like Caesar himself.

Caesar had one major health problem. He suffered from epilepsy – fainting fits. Apart from that he was incredibly fit for most of his life. When he was a teenager, Caesar used to train every day at the Campus Martius. Here he and the other boys would practise sports like wrestling and discus throwing, that are still played today. They would also play a number of ball games, using balls like our modern footballs made of hexagonal pieces of leather sewn together and then blown up.

Even in his forties and early fifties, he was fitter than many of his troops who were half his age. He fought most of his battles on foot, in the front line of his troops. There are stories that if the army came to a river, Caesar would jump in and swim, or float across on animal skins, and he was often the first to get to the other side.

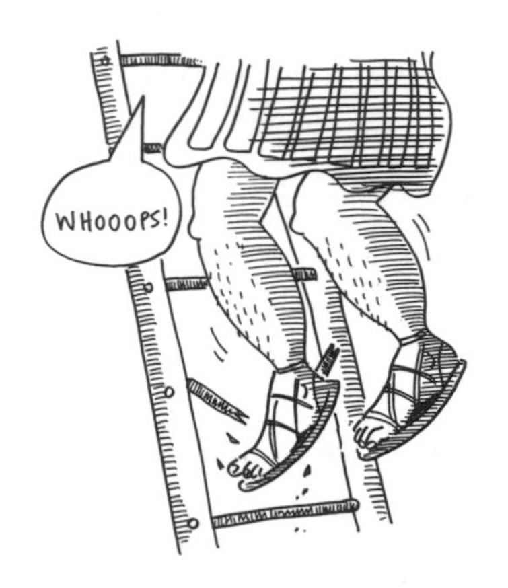

WHAT NEXT?

Caesar still couldn't pay back the enormous debts he'd accumulated. Only one of the very top jobs, being one of the two consuls, could wipe out those kinds of debts, and maybe satisfy Caesar's ambition.

But although Caesar had done very well, he still didn't have enough influence or power to stand a chance of being elected consul. Getting to the top in Rome was very much like climbing a ladder. All the steps were already set out and you had to follow them one at a time. Just like a ladder, if you tried to miss out three rungs, and jump instead of climb, you could find yourself in a lot of trouble. Caesar could see, from the example that Pompey had set, exactly what he had to do next.

POMPEY

Pompey was the most famous and powerful general in the Roman army. This was how he did it...

Pompey's golden rules for being top general:

• Always be on the winning side

In the civil war, Pompey started as a Marius supporter, then changed sides when it became obvious that Sulla was going to win.

• Know when to be loyal to the boss

Sulla sent Pompey to fight the supporters of Marius who had fled to Sicily and North Africa. Many surrendered to Pompey, expecting their old friend to be merciful. They were wrong. Pompey executed them all. Pompey became known as 'Sulla's butcher'. Sulla was very grateful.

• Know when to stand up to the boss

Sulla wasn't grateful *enough.* Pompey wanted a triumph – a

victory parade through the streets of Rome – as a reward for defeating the supporters of Marius. Sulla refused, so Pompey marched his troops to Rome and camped outside the city walls until Sulla gave in.

Lesson that Caesar learned from Pompey:	Caesar's next goal:
• Leading an army means never having to say that you're sorry.	• To be a governor of an important province, and to command his own army.

BACK IN THE ARMY

Once again, Caesar got the job he wanted: governor of Spain. The only problem was, the moneylenders he owed money to wouldn't let him leave Rome. They believed that if they let Caesar leave Rome, they would never see their money again.

Caesar desperately started searching for someone – anyone – who could get him off the hook, and out of Rome. He found him.

Crassus was Rome's richest slum-landlord. As people from the provinces streamed into Rome looking for work or the dole, men like Crassus built high-rise blocks of flats, called *insulae*, to house them. Often, these insulae were so hurriedly and badly built that they fell down, killing everyone inside. Crassus had an unusual method for buying land and houses to rebuild. He would wait for a fire to break out, then he would offer the owners of the burning house –

and the owners of all the neighbouring houses – a knock-down price to sell their houses on the spot. At one time or another, it was said, Crassus had owned most of Rome.

He'd also commanded armies. In 72BC a slave revolt, led by a gladiator named Spartacus, had started in Capua and quickly spread to Rome. The Senate made Crassus commander-in-chief. He defeated Spartacus and then crucified 6,000 of the rebels along the sides of the main road from Rome to Capua, as a warning to any other slaves who might have been thinking of rebelling.

Crassus agreed to help Caesar now, if Caesar helped *him* in the future.

Crassus promised Caesar's creditors that whatever happened to Caesar, he (Crassus) would pay off at least a quarter of all the money Caesar owed. This was good enough for the moneylenders. Caesar was allowed to leave Rome to take up his new job.

Army life was the life that Caesar loved best. From boyhood he'd always enjoyed physical sports. Away from the soft life of Rome, Caesar's body got leaner and fitter and his mind got tougher.

Caesar knew that this was his big opportunity to become

a really big shot. The Spanish legions, like the other legions of the Roman army, had no real loyalty to the city of Rome. Most of the legionnaires had never seen Rome; many had Spanish 'wives' and children (even though they weren't supposed to). And the oath of loyalty they took when they joined the Roman army was not to the empire or to the Senate but to the commander of their legion.

The only senators the soldiers trusted were their commanders, but only if those commanders gave them what they wanted – loot. And the only way to get loot was to have a good war against a weaker enemy.

Caesar did just what his soldiers wanted. As soon as he arrived in Spain he made sure the army was properly equipped and fighting fit, and then invaded Portugal. It was his chance to give his troops what they wanted (and a chance to grab some of the loot for himself too).

Caesar and his army marched across Portugal killing and stealing all the way. Even towns that surrendered were looted and burned.

At the end of his year as governor of Spain, Caesar had the loyalty of the Spanish legions, *and* he'd been awarded a triumph by the Senate in recognition of his victories.

TO TRIUMPH OR NOT TO TRIUMPH?

Caesar was a vain man, and a triumph was the greatest honour that could be given to a Roman general. It was a procession through the streets of Rome that officially declared: "This person is a hero". To a Roman it was like winning an Olympic gold medal, an Oscar and being interviewed on national television all rolled into one.

On the day of his triumph, the victorious general rode into Rome, at the head his troops, surrounded by cheering crowds. Behind the legions came a display of the loot they'd

captured, laid out on wagons and carts for the people of Rome to marvel at. Right at the end of the procession came the prisoners who had been captured and would be executed in public at the end of the triumph.

It was such a head-swelling experience that the rules said that a triumphant general had to have a slave riding in his chariot with him whose sole job was to whisper in the general's ear, "Remember – you are mortal!"

Caesar should have been delighted to be awarded a triumph, but he wasn't. Caesar had a big problem.

The rules of the triumph were very strict. A triumphant general was not allowed to come into the city until the day of the triumph itself. At any other time this would not have been a problem for Caesar, but just before the agreed date for Caesar's triumph, the elections for consul were to be held.

All the money Caesar had borrowed, all the crawling and flattering he'd done, all the battles he'd fought, had all been leading up to one thing – to be elected one of the two consuls of Rome.

Caesar knew he stood his best chance in these particular elections. He'd won the support of the people by providing wonderful shows; he'd won the support of the populare senators with bribes and promises; he'd won the loyalty of the Spanish legions; and now he was a great popular hero. Things would never be this good again.

But the rules of the election were as strict as the rules of the triumph. All candidates for election had to be present in the city during the election, and the election for consul was to be held *before* his triumph. What could Caesar do? If he accepted the triumph he couldn't stand for consul; if he entered the election for consul he would have to give up the triumph, the greatest day of any Roman's life.

After turning it over and over in his mind, Caesar decided to give up the triumph and enter the contest to become consul. He won.

Caesar was now the joint prime minister for a year – the most important man in Rome. (There was another consul, of course, a man named Bibulus, but when he left home to go to the Senate, Caesar's supporters threw dung at him! In the end, Bibulus just stayed home leaving Caesar to run everything.)

Surely now Caesar had everything he wanted, and could do anything he wanted.

NO.

TRIUMVIRATE

One of the best things about being consul happened at the end of the year, when you were given a province to rule.

But the Senate didn't want to give Caesar an important province to rule. Caesar was already too powerful for their liking. If Caesar became a ruler of an important province the senators all knew what he'd do – start a war, make lots of money from looting, and come back to Rome even more famous and even more powerful.

The Senate offered Caesar 'Italian woods and cattle tracks' to rule after his year as consul:

CAESAR : 0 SENATE : 1

Caesar was furious, but he didn't give up. He got Crassus to help him. They bribed and persuaded as many senators as they could. But they still didn't have enough power to get Caesar what he wanted:

CAESAR & CRASSUS : 1
SENATE : 1

Then Caesar did something brilliant. He added one more person to his alliance – Rome's most powerful general, Pompey.

Pompey: *While you're consul, will you give my retired soldiers land to live on?*

Caesar: *Always happy to help the army! And to show we're really good friends, you can marry my daughter Julia.*

Pompey joined the alliance with Caesar and Crassus, which became known as the *Triumvirate*, the Latin word meaning 'three rulers'.

CAESAR & CRASSUS & POMPEY : 2
SENATE : 1

GAUL

With the help of Pompey and Crassus, Caesar ended up being governor of *three* provinces: the area to the east of Rome; Northern Italy; and, best of all from Caesar's point of view, southern Gaul (southern France). Caesar now had his own empire of more than 320,000 square kilometres to do what he liked with, and with a bonus – the Senate had been forced to make him Governor for five years, not the usual one.

Caesar was now ruler of southern Gaul, but most of Germany, Belgium, France and Switzerland was independent, although linked to Rome by treaties.

THE GALLIC WARS LASTED FOR SEVEN YEARS.

To make sure everyone heard of his exploits, Caesar recorded the whole war in a book he wrote: *De Bel Gallico* (On the Gallic War). He wrote it in the third person, speaking of himself as 'Caesar' and not 'I' and 'me', so it reads like another person's account of Caesar's victories. As you can probably guess, it's full of tales of Caesar's bravery, Caesar's cunning and Caesar's brilliance.

Caesar made no secret of the fact that entire tribes were slaughtered, towns and villages destroyed and whole populations enslaved.

So ended the battle by which the tribe was almost annihilated and their name almost blotted out from the face of the earth...

Caesar decided to make an example of them... he had all their councillors executed and the rest of the population sold as slaves.

Caesar sold off an entire district of the town in one lot. The dealers gave him a receipt for 53,000 people...

Caesar remained in their territory for a few days, burning all the villages and cutting down the crops...

Caesar decided to make an example of them to deter the rest. He spared the lives of those who had taken up arms against him, but cut off their hands, a punishment intended to demonstrate clearly the evil of their ways...

Caesar even reached Britain, leading two raids in 55BC and 54BC. But he was never out of touch with what was going on in Rome. All through the Gallic Wars, Caesar often travelled to the borders of Italy to meet either Pompey or Crassus. They did various deals. For example, Pompey and Crassus made sure that Caesar got an extension on his governorship. In return, Caesar sent some of his troops to Rome on leave so that they could vote for Pompey and Crassus in the next elections for consuls. Fairly unsurprisingly, the two of them were elected.

END OF THE TRIUMVIRATE

Although the arrangement between Caesar, Pompey and Crassus seemed to be working well, it didn't last.

SOL 54BC

TRAGIC DEATH OF POMPEY'S WIFE

Julia, wife of top politician Pompey and only daughter of Caesar, conquerer of Gaul, dies in childbirth.

Her husband was old enough to be her father! Did Caesar sell his daughter for support against the Senate?

Will Caesar and Pompey stay friends now they're no longer family?

AND TODAY in your sensational, soaraway Sol... Page III sensation Tiresias – is he for real???

Now he had no family tie to Caesar, the optimate senators started trying to persuade Pompey to turn against Caesar. Then Crassus was killed.

IN DIES LUDUS 53BC

Crassus killed in Asia Minor

TOP TRIUMVIRATE TERMINATED!

Millionaire builder and soldier skewered somewhere in Syria – *Ouch!*

See back page for latest gladiator results

But Pompey was as ambitious and proud as Caesar. Pompey was used to being top general in Rome. Caesar's victories – which Pompey had helped bring about through his support – now threatened Pompey's own position.

In Dies Speculum 53BC

CAESAR AND POMPEY BATTLE TO BE BOSS

Allies on collision course: While Caesar stays in Gaul, optimate senators are busy trying to win over Pompey to the anti-Caesar camp. But Senate insiders say: "Beware of Pompey! Nothing less than being dictator will satisfy either Caesar or Pompey!"

The Senate saw its chance to disgrace Caesar. It drew up a list of charges against Caesar, crimes he was said to have committed while he was Consul. One of the crimes he was accused of was theft on a vast scale.

November 27th 51BC

In Dies Speculum

I CAME! I SAW! I BURGLED!

FAKE GOLD BAR SCANDAL ROCKS ROME!

Optimates claim: "Caesar to blame"

As senators continue to investigate Caesar's crimes when he was Consul, way back in 59BC, it's been claimed that a number of gold bars in the state treasury have turned out to be bronze painted to look like gold. All fingers have pointed at Caesar.

Senators – including Pompey, Caesar's old ally – are demanding that Caesar comes back to Rome from his estates in southern Gaul to stand trial.

The Senators who opposed Caesar – most of them – demanded that Caesar come to Rome in order to stand trial. Pompey agreed.

Caesar absolutely refused to come to Rome. But the senators wanted to disgrace Caesar, nothing else would satisfy them. Every time Caesar suggested a compromise, the senators refused. Eventually, after months of arguing, Caesar marched his legions into Italy, crossing the boundary of the River Rubicon, to fight it out with Pompey and the senators.

IN DIES SPECULUM

Jan 11 49BC

CIVIL WAR!

CAESAR CROSSES THE RIVER RUBICON SENATORS FLEE TO GREECE

Italian cities near the border with Gaul were today hurriedly building walls and ditches to try and keep out the legions of Caesar. Having seen what he did in Gaul, no-one's taking any chances! Worried citizens are asking: "Will Pompey protect us ?"

CIVIL WAR OR WORLD WAR?

If you look up civil war in the dictionary, it will tell you it's a war fought within a country between groups of citizens from that country. But this civil war wasn't fought in just one country, it was fought across the whole Roman empire, between troops from almost every nation in the empire.

As Caesar marched his troops through Italy many people packed up and fled; they knew how Caesar had treated the Gauls! Most of the Senators fled to Greece. Some Italian towns built hasty defences – walls and ditches – to try and keep Caesar and his army out.

But as he marched through Italy, Caesar did something

very clever. He *didn't* order his troops to burn the towns they captured, and he didn't have his opponents killed. He merely asked the people in the towns he captured to promise not to fight against him. Soon, many towns were welcoming Caesar as a hero.

Cicero, one of Caesar's most bitter opponents, complained:

"The country towns are treating him like a god... What honours these towns offer him! They are delighted with the cunning kindness of Caesar! "

Pompey went to Greece with his army; but he wasn't running away. Pompey knew that Caesar's army would have to get all its food and supplies sent all the way from Italy, because Greece was controlled by the senators who were Caesar's bitterest enemies. Pompey thought that if he forced Caesar's army to follow him to Greece, they'd run out of food and weapons *and* be outnumbered. Pompey was absolutely sure he could destroy Caesar.

The two great armies met at a place called Pharsalus. Caesar had 22,000 men, Pompey 45,000. The night before the battle, Pompey and his officers were so confident they'd win the battle they sat up most of the night arguing about how they would share all Caesar's wealth – who would get which of Caesar's villas; who would get his best farms and olive groves. They didn't think Caesar stood a chance. They were wrong.

Caesar was an expert on warfare. He'd carefully studied Pompey's usual tactics. Every time Pompey moved his infantry forward, Caesar's troops were there, waiting for him. It must have seemed to Pompey as if Caesar were a mind-reader. Whatever Pompey tried to do, Caesar anticipated him. Pompey's mighty army was destroyed – 15,000 of his men were killed and 24,000 were captured (more than Caesar's whole army!)

Pompey escaped, and fled to Egypt to try and raise a new army. Caesar chased after him. But when Caesar arrived at the Egyptian port of Alexandria, the Egyptian boy king, Ptolemy, sent him a special present – Pompey's head.

CARRYING ON WITH CLEO

Caesar stayed on in Egypt, fighting battles and falling in love with Cleopatra, Ptolemy's sister. When he finally returned to Rome in 46BC, he demanded – and got – four Triumphs. There was a whole month of celebrations, at the end of which Caesar was made dictator, for ten years, not the usual six months.

But after the celebrations came the reality of being in charge. Rome and the Empire was in a mess – much of it caused by Caesar and the civil war. Caesar was now the only real power in Rome, so he had to try and sort out the mess. The Senate still met, but no-one – least of all Caesar – paid any attention to its debates.

The first thing Caesar did was to reward his soldiers. As he'd promised, he gave his veterans land – land he'd confiscated from rich men who'd been on the losing side in the civil war. Then he rebuilt the ruined cities and created new towns of retired legionnaires in Greece and North Africa.

When he'd finished rewarding the army, Caesar started reorganising Roman life. He wrote new laws and developed a new calendar of 365 days with a leap year every four years. Helped by just a few friends – especially Mark Antony, who became Consul – Caesar worked from dawn till dusk. Sometimes, according to Suetonius, Caesar dictated four letters at a time to four different secretaries while at the same time reading complicated state papers!

FOOD FOR THOUGHT

For the first time in his life, Caesar started to suffer from long periods of bad health. He was working too hard, but he was also eating at far too many banquets.

The army food which Caesar had eaten as a young man was, even by our modern standards, a very well-balanced, healthy diet. The staple food was wheat, which the soldiers ground themselves and made into wholemeal porridge, bread or biscuits. This was eaten with vegetables, cheese, some fish, a little meat – usually bacon, olive oil and rough wine. In fact, on several occasions when the wheat ration was short and they had to eat more meat instead, the soldiers complained.

Roman breakfast (*frumentum*) and lunch (*prandium*) were also quite light and healthy meals. But the formal Roman banquets were becoming marathons of greed. Romans feasted lying down on three couches around a large square table. They didn't use knives and forks, but ate with their fingers (slaves came round after every course to wash the diners' hands). A Roman feast was a mixture of meal and cabaret, with jugglers, dancers and acrobats entertaining the guests between courses. And by the time Caesar became dictator, the food itself had to be part of the entertainment;

hosts tried to devise more and more exotic, unusual (and often indigestible) dishes.

Petronius, a Roman writing after Caesar's death, describes a feast that included pastry eggs with songbirds in the 'yolks', and sows udders stewed in fish sauce. But the high point of the meal was when a pack of hunting dogs burst into the dining room followed by a group of slaves carrying a huge roast boar. When one of the slaves cut open the bulging belly of the boar, live thrushes flew out of it which were caught in nets by the other slaves and offered to the guests as appetisers before they ate the roast boar itself.

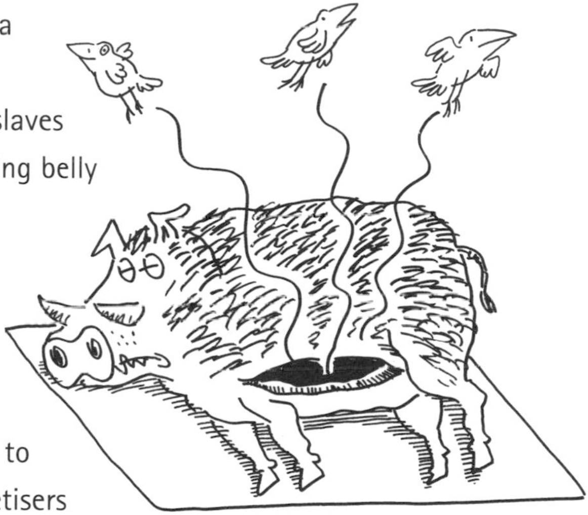

Like many wealthy Romans, Caesar loved feasting and was known to take emetics – potions like salt water to make himself sick – before a big meal so that he could eat even more. No wonder his health was poor if he was vomiting, then gorging himself, and then repeating the same thing the next day, and the day after that.

THE FATAL MISTAKE

When Caesar was made dictator, he increased the number of senators from 600 to 900 so that he could reward some of his less politically powerful friends by making them senators. He also gave citizenship to non-Italians.

The changes to the Senate and to the laws of citizenship were too much for many of the old senators, especially the optimates. They were certain now that Caesar would never be satisfied until he'd destroyed the Republic and had himself made king. Caesar, in his determination to sort out Rome's problems ignored them, but the senators were not as powerless as he thought.

In February 44BC, Caesar made his fatal mistake – he had himself proclaimed *Dictator for Life*.

This was the last straw for the Senate, even for several senators who had previously been Caesar's supporters and friends. Trying to become king was a crime which was punishable by death. Although Caesar publicly refused a crown when Mark Antony offered it to him, Caesar was now a king in all but name.

A group of senators decided to take the law into their own hands. They knew that the only way to stop Caesar was to kill him; and they decided that it was their duty to do so.

Caesar was to attend a meeting of the Senate on 15th March – what the Romans called the 'Ides of March'. He'd been unwell and his wife, Calpurnia, pleaded with him not to go. She claimed to have had bad dreams – omens of death. Other strange signs had been seen foretelling doom. A fortune-teller had told Caesar that something bad would happen to him on the Ides of March. Caesar ignored them all.

The Senate was being rebuilt, to accommodate all the new senators, so the meeting of the Ides of March was to take place in the great stone theatre which had been built on the Campus Martius by Pompey.

Caesar pushed his way through the crowd gathered around the theatre. He saw the fortune-teller.

"The Ides of March are here," said Caesar.

"But not ended," replied the fortune-teller.

Caesar entered a long colonnade which led to the hall behind the stage where the Senate meeting was to take place. Before he could leave the colonnade, Caesar was surrounded by a group of 23 senators. Each produced a dagger and – as agreed – so that no-*one* would be to blame, they all stabbed. Most of the wounds were just scratches, and in the melee some senators cut each other, but one dagger plunged deep into Caesar's chest. Seeing his friend Brutus he groaned, "Not you too, Brutus!" Then, in shame at his weakness, or maybe in imitation of a priest at a sacrifice, Caesar pulled his toga over his head, slumped to the floor and died.

Standing above him, like a witness to his destruction, was a marble statue of his old ally and murdered rival, Pompey.

FRIENDS, ROMANS, COUNTRYMEN...

Many people today still believe that Caesar was the greatest of heroes; a strong man who was not afraid to start wars – even civil wars – to fulfil his ambition to make the Roman Empire even bigger, and to rule it alone. Kings, emperors and modern dictators have admired Caesar and taken him as an example to follow. Some rulers have even tried to suggest that they were in some way his direct descendents. For example, the words *tsar* (the title of the Russian emperors before 1917) and *Kaiser* (the German monarchs until 1918) are both versions of the name Caesar.

Others take the opposite view. One modern writer has calculated that around two million men, women and children died in the Gallic War. This would make Caesar one of the greatest mass-murderers and war criminals in history.

What can't be denied is that Caesar was one of the few men to almost single-handedly change the course of world history. If you try to imagine what would have happened if there had been no Julius Caesar you'll see what I mean.

Without Caesar the Empire might have fallen apart. He set the example of being a military dictator which the later emperors followed.

As the first emperors were Caesar's sucessors and members of his own family, without Caesar there would have been no Roman royal family and no emperors.

Without Caesar Gaul and Britain might not have been invaded, and Britain would not have become part of the Empire. Britain might have stayed a Celtic country of small tribes, and not been united under Rome.

Many British, European and American laws are Roman in origin, or follow the example of Roman laws. Even the calendar we now use is based on the one Caesar invented. We might have had none of these without Caesar.

Without Caesar's example to follow, there might have been no tsars or kaisers; no Napoleon and no Mussolini. And without those empires, there might have been no first or second World War.

Europe and the world might have been a much better place without Caesar and the Roman Empire, or it might have been worse: it would certainly have been very different.

If that sort of influence is what people mean when they describe Caesar as a "great man" they're probably right. But whether Caesar was a good man or a bad man... that's for you to decide for yourself.

titles in the series

Spilling the Beans on Albert Einstein

Spilling the Beans on Charles Darwin

Spilling the Beans on Julius Caesar

Spilling the Beans on Robin Hood

Spilling the Beans on Tutankhamen

Spilling the Beans on William Shakespeare